COUNTRY FACT FILES

SWEDEN

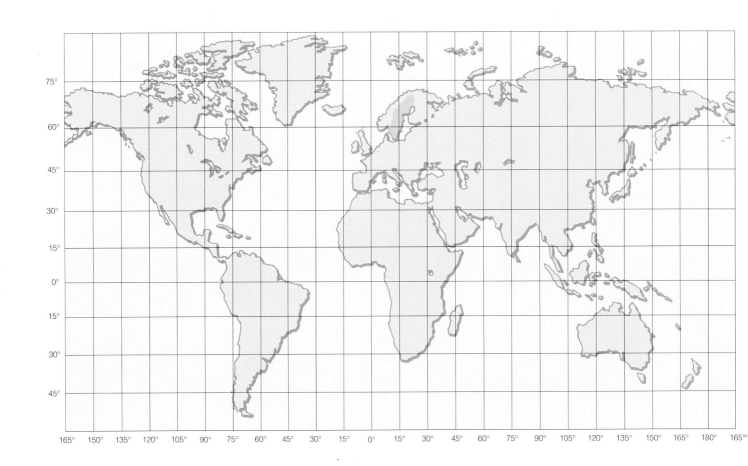

ARCTIC OCEAN

N
W E
S

0   200 km
0   120 mi

Arctic Circle

NORWEGIAN

SEA

• Narvik

• Kiruna

• Gällivare

• Luleå

S W E D E N

• Umeå

G U L F   O F   B O T H N I A

• Östersund

FINLAND

• Sundsvall

NORWAY

• Gävle

60°

• Uppsala
Västerås •

Örebro •   ■
     STOCKHOLM

Lake Vänern

UTÖ

Lake Vättern

Norrköping •

Linköping •

B A L T I C   S E A

ESTONIA

• Göteborg

Jönköping •

Visby •
GOTLAND

NORTH

LATVIA

SEA

Kalmar •
ÖLAND

LITHUANIA

• Hälsingborg
• Lund
• Malmö

DENMARK

ÖRESUND

POLAND

RUSSIAN
FED.

15°

SWEDEN

Bo Kage Carlson

RSVP
RAINTREE
STECK-VAUGHN
PUBLISHERS
A Steck-Vaughn Company

Austin, Texas

Published by Raintree Steck-Vaughn Publishers,
an imprint of Steck-Vaughn Company

Design and typesetting	Roger Kohn Designs
Commissioning editor	Rosie Nixon
Editor	Merle Thompson
Picture research	Shelley Noronha
Maps	János Márffy

We are grateful to the following for permission
to reproduce photographs:
Front cover: Robert Harding, *above* (K. Hart); Britstock, *below* (Hans Stroud); B & C Alexander, pages 9, 12 *below right,* 14, 14/15, 19, 38, 42; Britstock, page 10 *below left* (Hans Strand); Bruce Coleman, pages 13 (J. Jurka), 15 (J. Jurka), 32 (J. Jurica); C M Dixon, page 8 *above center*; Genesis, page 43; Leslie Garland, pages 11 *bottom right*, 16, 28/29 *below right*, 36 *below left*; Robert Harding, pages 7 (M. Jenner), 29 *above right* (C. Andreason), 31 (C. Andreason), 37; Papillo, pages 10/11 *above center*, 22 *below right*; Pica Press, pages 18 (B. Larsson-Ask), 22 *above left* (B. Larsson-Ask), 23 (A. Wiklund), 24 (J. Henriksson), 25 (J. Henriksson), 26 (P. Ulf), 27 *above left* (P. Ydreskog), 27 *below right* (J. Holzer), 28 *above left* (P. Flato), 30 (M. Lundberg), 33 (L. R. Jansson), 34 (C. Jonson), 35 (T. Sica), 36 *above right* (G. Ludmark), 39; 40/41; Tony Stone, 8 *below center* (L. Gullachsen), 12 *above left* (C. Ehlers), 20 (T. Wood); WPL, page 21.

The statistics given in this book are the most up-to-date available
at the time of going to press.

Printed in Hong Kong by Wing King Tong

Library of Congress Cataloging-in-Publication Data
Carlson, Bo Kage, 1939–
Sweden/Bo Kage Carlson.
p.   cm. — (Country fact files)
Includes bibliographical references and index.
Summary: Introduces the landscape, climate, natural resources, people, daily life, government, and economy of the northern European country of Sweden.
ISBN 0-8172-5407-2
1. Sweden — Juvenile literature.   [1. Sweden.]   I. Title.   II. Series.
DL609.C37   1999
984.5 — dc21   98-31485
CIP
AC

1 2 3 4 5 6 7 8 9 0 HK 02 01 00 99 98

CONTENTS

Words that are explained in the glossary are printed in
SMALL CAPITALS the first time they are mentioned in the text.

Modern Sweden is a highly industrialized country, and its people enjoy an excellent standard of living. This, however, is a recent development that did not begin until the end of the 19th century.

The country was first settled some 13,000 years ago, when the last ICE AGE was coming to an end. First to arrive were reindeer hunters, who came from the European continent across a land bridge connecting Denmark with Sweden. They were followed by fishermen, herdsmen, and, eventually, by farmers. They gradually spread through the full length of the country, but even today Sweden is thinly populated. This is especially true of the northern part of the country, where the climate is severe.

The first Swedes lived in small communities, but gradually a number of kingdoms were formed. Most people made a poor living from the land. From the 9th to the 12th centuries, some, known as Vikings, left their homes for long periods traveling by ship to trade, to plunder, or to find new land. Many found their way to England and France, while others sailed down the Russian rivers as far as Turkey and Greece.

In about A.D. 1000, the smaller kingdoms were united into one country. Stockholm became its capital in about

▼ *Riddarholmen (Knights' Island) in central Stockholm, with the old town and the Royal Castle in the background.*

◀ *A memorial stone at Alskog on the island of Gotland. It shows the eight-legged horse of the Viking god Odin.*

1250. Swedish kings also ruled over Finland for hundreds of years and, for a briefer period, over Norway. Since 1905, however, Sweden has not had any overseas colonies or departments. But there are millions of people of Swedish origin living abroad. This is because, from about 1850 to 1950, approximately 1.5 million people emigrated to other countries, especially to America, to escape poverty.

Because industrialization arrived late in Sweden, in 1900, 75 percent of the people still lived in the countryside. During the 20th century, Sweden has rapidly changed into an industrial country with over 80 percent of its inhabitants living in urban areas. Today Sweden is best known for its Volvo cars and Ericsson telephone systems.

▲ *A Lapp (Sami) herdsman using a snow scooter to keep up with his herd of reindeer. The Lapp people live mainly in northern Sweden.*

SWEDEN AT A GLANCE

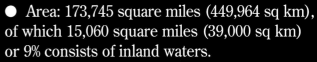

● Area: 173,745 square miles (449,964 sq km), of which 15,060 square miles (39,000 sq km) or 9% consists of inland waters.
● Population: (1997) 8.9 million
● Population density: 52 per square mile (19.8 per sq km)
● Capital: Stockholm, population (1997) 727,000 (Greater Stockholm has a population of 1.75 million.)
● Other main cities (1997): Göteborg 457,000; Malmö 251,000; Uppsala 186,000
● Highest mountain: Mount Kebnekaise, 6,925 feet (2,111 m)
● Largest lake: Vänern, 2,182 square miles (5,650 sq km)
● Longest river: Torne älv, 316 miles (510 km)
● Language: Swedish
● Major religion: Christianity (87% of Swedes are members of the Lutheran church.)
● Life expectancy: 79 years (81 years for women and 76 years for men)
● Currency: Swedish crowns (kronor), written as SEK. The krona is divided into 100 öre.
● Economy: Highly industrialized. Less than 3% of the workforce is employed in agriculture and fishing.
● Major resources: Iron ore, timber, hydro-electricity, nuclear power
● Major products: Cars and other engineering products, electronic equipment, paper, and pulp
● Environmental problems: Air pollution in the larger cities; water pollution from shipping, industry, and agriculture

THE LANDSCAPE

Sweden is one of the largest countries in Europe. It covers about two-thirds of the Scandinavian Peninsula. It is long and narrow, stretching almost 995 miles (1,600 km) from north to south, but only 310 miles (500 km) from east to west. Its land border with Norway to the west is 995 miles (1,600 km) long, while the border with Finland to the east stretches for 350 miles (560 km). A narrow strait, Öresund, less than 2.5 miles (4 km) wide, separates it from Denmark to the southwest.

The coastline is 995 miles (1,600 km) long, and there are several groups of islands or archipelagos. The largest group lies to the east of Stockholm. There are also larger islands, such as Gotland and Öland, in the Baltic Sea.

A long mountain range runs along the border with Norway. Some peaks reach a height of 6,560 feet (2,000 m). These were once much higher, but they were eroded away during the ice age by the rocks and boulders carried in the ice. As

◀ *More than half of Sweden is covered by forests, and thousands of lakes dot the landscape. In the north, there are many mountains that have rounded summits.*

◀ A village in a clearing in the forest. It overlooks a fertile plain, a landscape that is typical in Sweden.

one of the most densely forested countries in Europe.

Several large rivers run from the mountains along the borders toward the Baltic Sea. There are also a number of rivers carrying water from the southern highlands. Most rivers have been dammed to provide hydroelectricity, but a few have been preserved for environmental reasons.

The Swedish landscape is dotted with lakes. Most of these are small, but 4,000 of them cover areas larger than a square mile. Some are very large, especially Lake Vänern, which is the third largest lake in Europe after Lake Ladoga and Lake Onega in Russia.

the ice melted, sediment was deposited in the lowland areas, turning them into fertile plains.

To the south and along the coast, there are large, lowland plains separated by somewhat higher forest areas, the South Swedish Highlands. About 55 percent of Sweden is covered by forests, making it

▼ A view from the mountaintop of Sulitelma. It overlooks Padjelanta National Park, the largest of Sweden's 24 national parks.

KEY FACTS

● The largest lakes are Vänern, 2,180 square miles (5,648 sq km); Vättern, 738 square miles (1,912 sq km); Mälaren, 440 square miles (1,140 sq km); and Hjälmaren, 185 square miles (478 sq km).
● Several of the lakes are very deep. Hornavan is 725 feet (221 m), Torneträsk 550 feet (168 m), Siljan 440 feet (134 m), and Vättern 420 feet (128 m) deep.
● Together Klarälven, Lake Vänern, and Göta älv form a natural waterway 403 miles (650 km) long, 100 miles (160 km) of which run through Norway.
● Some of Sweden's mountain peaks may well have been as high as those in the Himalayas before they eroded.

Sweden lies as far north as Siberia and Alaska, areas with an Arctic or near-Arctic climate, and as far south as Denmark. Therefore, the climate in southern Sweden is very different from that of the north. For example, it is warm enough for people in the south of the country to begin going to the beach in late May or early June. In the mountains of northwest Lapland, however, people would still be using their skis and skates.

Summers north of the Arctic Circle are short, but the hours of daylight are very long. In the summer, the midnight sun does not dip below the horizon.

In the winter, however, the days are very short. In the extreme north, for about two weeks around Christmas, the sun never reaches above the horizon. The variations in daylight between summer and winter are much less notable in southern Sweden. Winters in the north are much colder than in the south. In the extreme north, the average January temperature is 18 to 27°F (10 to 15°C) below that of the south. In July the difference is only 4 to 5°F (2 to 3°C).

The long winters in northern Sweden

▲ *Picnickers in Stockholm on a pleasant summer day are watching a yacht race taking place on Lake Riddarfjärden. The City Hall is visible on the right in the background.*

▲ *The arrival of spring is celebrated all
over the country on Walpurgis Night, in
April, when bonfires are lit.*

KEY FACTS

● During the winter,
the whole country is
covered with snow.
In the northern
mountains, the snow is
40 to 80 inches (100 to
200 cm) deep and lasts
for 7 to 8 months. The south of the country
has a blanket of snow 8 to 16 inches (20 to
40 cm) deep that lasts for less than two
months.
● The highest temperature ever recorded
in Sweden is 100°F (38°C). The lowest
ever, –63°F (–53°C), was reported in
December 1941, from Malgovik, in Lapland.
● Stockholm is on approximately the same
latitude as Churchill, Manitoba, in Canada.

mean that the growing season is very
short. In some parts of Lapland, there
are only 100 days a year when the
temperature is high enough for plants
to grow. This makes farming extremely
difficult. In the southern third of the
country, however, plants can grow for
about 200 days each year.

Because of the Gulf Stream, which
brings warm water and mild winds from
the West Indies across the Atlantic
Ocean, most of Sweden has a mild
climate. In Stockholm, located 60° north
of the equator, the January average
temperature is 28°F (–2.5°C). The world's
average on that latitude is 5°F (–15°C).

Since the wind blows mainly from the

west, the west coast gets more rain than
other parts of the country. In some areas,
this is as much as 40 to 48 inches (100 to
120 cm) a year. The eastern coastal areas
receive only 24 to 28 inches (60 to 70 cm).
Some inland areas in the north receive
even less, because the clouds from the
west have deposited their rain over the
mountains along the border with Norway.

◀ *In Jukkasjärvi,
in Lapland, locals
as well as tourists
have to travel on
snow scooters.*

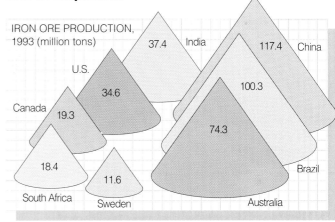

◀ *Iron ore is found underground in Sweden. Most of the deposits are in Lapland.*

IRON ORE PRODUCTION, 1993 (million tons)

India 37.4

China 117.4

U.S. 34.6

100.3

Canada 19.3

74.3

18.4

South Africa

11.6

Sweden

Brazil

Australia

Iron, wood, and water have for centuries been key elements in the development of Sweden and are still important to the modern Swedish economy. At first, iron ore was collected in swamps and lakes, but in the 12th century, production began to increase when the first iron ore mine was opened on the island of Utö, in the Baltic Sea. In the 19th century, the export of wood helped to finance the development of industries and railroads in Sweden. In the 20th century, rivers were dammed to provide electricity.

The major deposits of iron ore are in Lapland, near the towns of Kiruna, Gällivare, and Malmberget. Some of this ore is used to make iron and steel in Sweden, but most of it is exported. The iron ore is sent by rail to the Norwegian port of Narvik, because Swedish ports along the Gulf of Bothnia are frozen in the winter. Sweden also produces some gold, silver, and copper and exports refined zinc and lead.

KEY FACTS

● Of the total electricity supply, 52% is produced by hydroelectricity, 42% by nuclear power, and 6% from oil, coal, and other sources.

● Nuclear power is a controversial issue. Parliament decided to close down 1 reactor in 1998. The remaining 11 reactors will probably be gradually shut down within the next 20 years.

● There are 60 major power plants in Sweden. Of these, 45 are hydroelectric plants, and 4 are nuclear power generation plants, each with 2 to 4 reactors.

● Cheap energy is an important resource for some sectors of the industry, especially for factories that produce pulp and paper.

Timber, pulp, and paper make up 18 percent of the total exports. The most important timber-producing areas are in the southern half of the country, where trees grow faster than in the north.

Half the electricity that is consumed in Sweden comes from water power, and the rest is mainly from nuclear reactors. Because electricity is cheaper in Sweden than in most other countries, it is used to power industry and to heat the majority of the houses. Oil, however, still has to be imported. Over the next few decades, nuclear power will be phased out, so Sweden is now looking for alternative energy sources. New ways of producing energy are being explored, such as SUSTAINABLE FORESTS with fast-growing trees that can be used in special furnaces for generating electricity and heating.

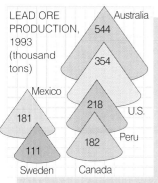

LEAD ORE PRODUCTION, 1993 (thousand tons)

Australia 544
354
Mexico
218
181
U.S.
111
182 Peru
Sweden   Canada

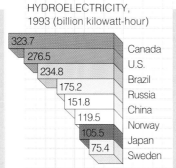

HYDROELECTRICITY, 1993 (billion kilowatt-hour)

323.7	Canada
276.5	U.S.
234.8	Brazil
175.2	Russia
151.8	China
119.5	Norway
105.5	Japan
75.4	Sweden

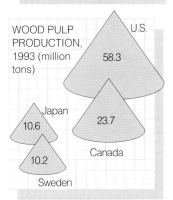

WOOD PULP PRODUCTION, 1993 (million tons)

U.S. 58.3
Japan 10.6
23.7
10.2
Canada
Sweden

◀ *The sawdust collected from sawmills such as this one is often used to make boards or fuel.*

▲ *Logging often takes place during the winter months. The frozen ground makes log transport easier.*

Compared to most countries, Sweden is not densely populated. It has an average of 52 inhabitants per square mile (20 per sq km). The population density, however, differs widely from north to south. In Lapland, there are only about 2.6 people per square mile (1 per sq km), but in the southern third of the country, where 80 percent of Swedes live, there are 125 people per square mile (48 per sq km).

Population growth is slow, with a natural increase of only a few thousand each year, from 0.1 to 0.2 percent. Immigration has, however, caused the population to increase at a higher rate than this in recent years.

At the end of the 19th century, people

◀ Drottninggatan is a long street for pedestrians in central Stockholm. It is a popular shopping place.

LIFE EXPECTANCY, 1995	
80	Japan
79	Sweden
79	China
78	Switzerland
78	France
78	Norway
78	Netherlands
78	Canada
78	Italy
78	Greece
77	Belgium
77	U.K.
77	U.S.
77	Australia
77	Austria
77	Ireland

▶ A residential area in Stockholm on the shore of Lake Mälaren, one of the largest lakes in Sweden.

began to move from rural areas to industrial towns and cities. Today 83 percent of Swedes live in urban areas. One-third of them have settled in and around the three largest cities—Stockholm, Göteborg, and Malmö.

The Swedish government has set up programs in the rural areas, the north, and on the islands to create more jobs. These have not been very successful in persuading people to stay. Young people, especially, leave because of better job opportunities in the cities.

The physical features of the Swedes do not differ much from the north to the south of the country. Although many are tall with light-colored hair, this is not always the case. There are many exceptions, since people have, for centuries, migrated to Sweden from other parts of the continent.

There are some small, long-established minorities. The largest minority group consists of some 30,000 Finnish-speaking inhabitants of the Torne älv River valley in

KEY FACTS

● Swedish is spoken in Finland by about 300,000 people, or 6% of the population. The biggest concentration of Swedish speakers is on the island of Åland and its archipelago, where Swedish is the official language. This is a result of six centuries of Swedish rule over Finland.

● The Swedish alphabet has three letters, å, ä, and ö, that do not exist in the English language. They come at the end of the Swedish alphabet, after z. The small dots and circles over the letters are important for correct pronunciation.

● Since 1954, a Nordic labor market has been established. This allows citizens of Denmark, Finland, Iceland, Norway, and Sweden to live and work in any of these countries without a work permit.

● Since 1995, Sweden has been a member of the European Union (EU), which allows citizens of any of its 15 member countries to work and live anywhere inside the EU.

● In 1749 Sweden became the first country in the world to keep detailed population statistics. From this date onward, records exist with the exact number of inhabitants in each town and village.

● Sweden's population growth: 0.9 million (1571); 1.4 million (1700); 2 million (1767); 3 million (1835); 4 million (1863); 5 million (1897); 6 million (1923); 7 million (1950); 8 million (1969); 8.9 million (1998).

the north. The Lapps, who number about 17,000, usually live in the mountains of northern Sweden. About 2,500 of them still make a living from herding reindeer. Others have moved to towns in search of jobs. There are also 20,000 Jews and 7,000 gypsies.

During the last few decades, the number of New Swedes (immigrants from other countries) has increased. Some of these New Swedes came in the period from about 1950 to 1980, looking for jobs. Most of them came from neighboring countries, especially Finland. Later, refugees fled to Sweden from wars in the Middle East, Africa, and the former Yugoslavia.

The arrival of large numbers of immigrants has caused some problems, especially in the suburbs of the big cities. There, people who look or dress differently feel that they are discriminated against.

Some of the more recent arrivals have

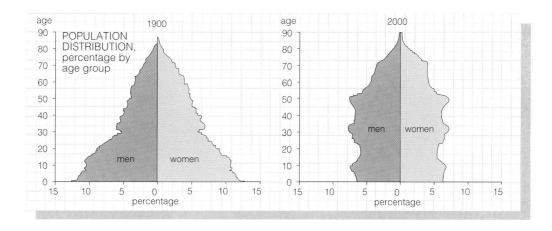

This photograph shows a ceremony welcoming immigrants to Hallunda, a suburb of Stockholm that has a large percentage of immigrants.

POPULATION DISTRIBUTION, percentage by age group

1900 — men / women

2000 — men / women

not been integrated as well as the earlier immigrants were. They often live together in the suburbs of the big cities. In the Stockholm area, one in six inhabitants was born outside of Sweden.

Today almost one in ten inhabitants of Sweden were born abroad. Many have become Swedish citizens. They can do this after they have lived in the country for five years. Others expect to return to their home countries when peace has been restored there. Most immigrants learn Swedish; this is essential if they are to get a job. Even so, unemployment among immigrants is high.

Swedish is the mother tongue for native Swedes. There are many dialects, but people can easily understand one another. Lapps have their own language, but most of them also speak Swedish. Finnish is still the language for most of the 200,000 people of Finnish origin living in Sweden.

Because Sweden is a small country and Swedish is rarely spoken outside its borders, all Swedish students learn English as a foreign language, starting at the age of nine or ten. Many also learn French, German, and other commonly spoken languages.

A Lapp posing in traditional costume with his prize-winning reindeer.

LEISURE

Because of the climate, people's lifestyle changes considerably from summer to winter. During the long, warm summer days, people spend a lot of time in the open air. But it is so cold and dark in the winter that people tend to use their spare time differently. For young people to make the most of the summer, there is a ten-week school vacation from early June to late August, whereas the winter breaks are very short.

Most Swedes enjoy outdoor life. City people often have a summer house, where they spend vacations and weekends. Often these houses are well insulated, so that they can also be used during the winter for skiing or long-distance skating trips. Because of the long coastline and the many islands, most people own a boat so that they can go sailing.

Access to the countryside is guaranteed by tradition and law. It was once important

for the poor to be able to pick berries and mushrooms to supplement an otherwise poor diet. Today everybody has access to privately owned forests and most other areas for walking, for picking berries, and for swimming. No one is allowed, however, to chop down trees or to go too close to inhabited houses. There are also laws restricting the exploitation of the seashore to keep it accessible to the public.

KEY FACTS

● Orienteering originated in Sweden. It combines skills in map reading and cross-country running. Today it is popular all over the world.

● Long-distance skating is very popular in those areas of Sweden where lakes, rivers, and the water around the groups of islands freeze during the winter.

● Forty percent of Swedes live in privately owned villas and terraced houses, 15% in privately owned apartments, and 45% in rented apartments and houses.

● In Sweden, 1 out of 3 people have access to the Internet via their telephones and computers.

WORK

The work week is generally 35 to 40 hours long, but many people, especially women, only work part-time. Swedes have a minimum of five weeks paid vacation each year in addition to public holidays.

EDUCATION

Since both parents often work, most children attend state or private nurseries from the age of about two. School is compulsory between the ages of 7 and 16, but many children start their education at age 6 and continue until they are 19.

There are private schools, but generally Swedish children are educated at schools run by local authorities. For the first nine years, everybody follows more or less the same curriculum. During the final two years, students can make some individual choices, such as learning an extra foreign language or studying a more advanced course of mathematics.

HOLIDAYS AND RELIGIOUS FESTIVALS	
January 1	NEW YEAR'S DAY
January 6	TWELFTH NIGHT (Epiphany)
March/April	EASTER
April 30	VALBORG, or WALPURGIS An ancient festival when bonfires are lit and students sing to greet the coming of spring.
May 1	LABOR DAY
May	ASCENSION DAY
Early June	PENTECOST
Late June	MIDSUMMER People traditionally dance around a maypole.
Early November	ALL SAINTS' DAY
December 13	LUCIA DAY (Festival of Light)
December 24–26	CHRISTMAS

More than nine out of ten students continue for another three years of school from the ages of 16 to 19, during which period they can choose between a number of options. Some study a program of academic subjects in preparation for university. Others take a mixture of

◄ *People enjoying a coffee and a chat in the medieval Stortorget (Great Square) in the old town of Stockholm.*

▶ *There are many women police officers in Sweden. Here, one has stopped to talk with a senior citizen.*

◀ A popular winter sport is bandy, a Scandinavian form of ice hockey played with curved sticks and a ball. The Swedish championship finals are some of the biggest sporting events of the year.

▶ Dogsled races are held on frozen lakes. They are especially popular during the long winters of northern Sweden.

academic and vocational subjects in order to become skilled workers, such as carpenters, car mechanics, or hairdressers.

Discipline problems are increasing in Swedish schools. This is partly because classes have become larger due to budget cuts, and also because a larger number of teenagers stay on at school today, including some who are poorly motivated.

Swedish classrooms are informal. Pupils always call their teachers by their first names. Since the 1960s, Swedes have stopped using formal methods of address in schools as well as in the workplace.

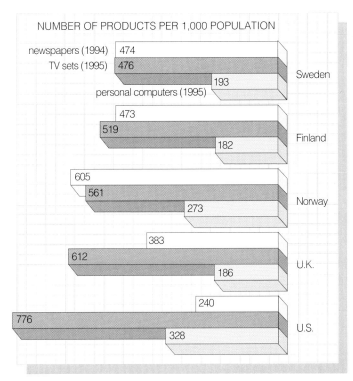

NUMBER OF PRODUCTS PER 1,000 POPULATION

newspapers (1994)	474	
TV sets (1995)	476	
		193 Sweden
personal computers (1995)		

	473	
	519	
		182 Finland

605		
561		
	273	Norway

	383	
612		
		186 U.K.

	240	
776		
	328	U.S.

Sports play an important part in the daily lives of Swedes. Soccer and ice hockey are the most popular sports and are played by most Swedish children, girls as well as boys. Others prefer tennis, table tennis, swimming, horse riding, orienteering, skiing, and skating. Adults often take up jogging, body building, and golf to stay fit.

Evening classes are very popular for both young people and adults. These are encouraged by government grants. People study such things as photography, art, chess, or foreign languages. Originally, evening classes were introduced by the

▼ *Roxette, one of many Swedish pop groups that has become popular abroad, performs in Helsinki.*

labor movement and the alcohol awareness organizations in the late 19th century to help poor and uneducated persons improve themselves. Today, at a time when people are better educated, the main purpose is to offer meaningful recreation activities and to keep young people occupied.

Almost every home has a television set, and most families have a personal computer. Many people spend several hours a day watching television and video cassettes or surfing the Internet.

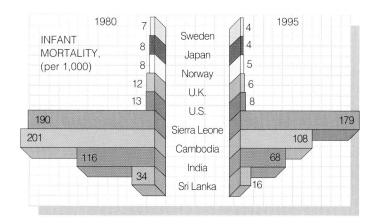

INFANT MORTALITY, (per 1,000)	1980		1995
Sweden	7		4
Japan	8		4
Norway	8		5
U.K.	12		6
U.S.	13		8
Sierra Leone	190		179
Cambodia	201		108
India	116		68
Sri Lanka	34		16

RELIGION

More than nine out of ten Swedes belong to a Christian church, but less than half practice their religion. The Lutheran Church, the state church of Sweden since the 16th century, is the largest of these. Other popular Protestant churches include

the Pentecostalist, Baptist, Methodist, and the Salvation Army. There are also 150,000 Catholics in Sweden, and several thousand immigrants from Greece, the former Yugoslavia, the Middle East, Russia, and Ukraine belong to Orthodox churches.

The largest non-Christian religion is Islam with some 130,000 followers. Most of them are immigrants from the Middle East. There are also about 20,000 Jews, 15,000 Buddhists, and 5,000 Hindus.

◀ *Children in a fourth-grade class perform an experiment during a science lesson at the Bombacka School, in Södertälje.*

▶ *In a ceremony held in Uppsala Cathedral in 1997, Christina Odelberg was consecrated as the first woman bishop of the Lutheran church in Sweden. In 1998 a second female bishop was appointed.*

Prime Minister Göran Persson (top center) with his cabinet at Harpsund, the official country retreat of the Swedish government.

THE GOVERNMENT
Prime Minister
About 20 ministers

RIKSDAGEN (Parliament)
Speaker
349 members

In recent elections 6 to 7 parties have been represented in Parliament.

"All public power comes from the people" (The Swedish Constitution). All Swedish citizens over the age of 18 have the right to vote in elections to Parliament and the provincial and local assemblies.

Sweden is one of the few remaining monarchies in Europe, but the king or queen has no political power, only a symbolic role. The prime minister and his or her ministers govern the country. Parliament has the power to make laws and decide on the budget, while the law courts are independent.

The Swedish Parliament, Riksdagen, first met in Arboga in 1435. It has gradually changed over the centuries to become more representative of the population as a whole. Riksdagen has 349 members in a single chamber. Elections to the Parliament and to regional and local assemblies take place every four years, and all Swedes have the right to vote from the age of 18.

Major political parties in Sweden are the Social Democrats, the Moderates, the Left Party, the People's Party, the Center Party, the Christian Democrats, and the Environmental Party.

KEY FACTS

● Women make up 40% of the members of Parliament. This is a higher percentage than that of any other country in the world.
● The election system is based on proportional representation, and each party presents the voters with a list of its candidates. A party with, for instance, 20% of the votes will have 20% of the seats in the Parliament. However, for a party to have members elected, it must receive a minimum of 4% of the total vote.
● Participation in elections is usually high. Generally 80 to 90% of those eligible to vote go to the polls.
● Sweden is a hereditary monarchy, and the crown is passed on to the eldest child. The present king, Carl Gustav XVI, will be succeeded by his daughter, Crown Princess Victoria.

◀ *Anna Maltinger, a 22-year-old Swedish air force pilot. She is one of a small but increasing number of women in the Swedish armed forces.*

communications, and they also run community services.

In 1809 the Swedish Parliament introduced the post of ombudsman. This is a Swedish word meaning "representative." The independence of this post is guaranteed by law and the constitution. The ombudsman's role is to hear complaints from the public and put a stop to corruption and the abuse of power by the central and local governments. This Swedish institution, and the word "ombudsman" has been adopted by many other countries. There are now several similar institutions in Sweden to which people can complain if they feel they have been unfairly treated by the media or discriminated against because of their sex or race.

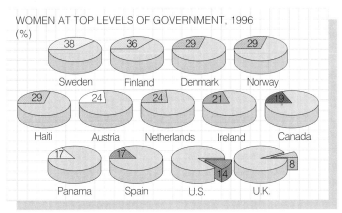

WOMEN AT TOP LEVELS OF GOVERNMENT, 1996
(%)

38	36	29	29
Sweden	Finland	Denmark	Norway

29	24	24	21	19
Haiti	Austria	Netherlands	Ireland	Canada

17	17	14	8
Panama	Spain	U.S.	U.K.

The country was, until recently, divided into 24 provinces, but a process is now under way to reorganize the provincial administration into larger units. There are 289 local communities of varying size, each of which has its local assembly. Provincial and local bodies decide on issues that pertain to hospitals, schools, and local

▶ *King Carl Gustav XVI shaking hands with President Nelson Mandela during a visit to South Africa, with former President F. W. de Klerk waiting his turn.*

FOOD AND FARMING

Food production in Sweden has undergone dramatic changes during the 20th century. This is particularly true of the period after World War II, when agriculture became more mechanized. In 1950, 25 percent of the Swedish workforce was employed in agriculture. Now it is only about 2.5 percent.

The land area used for farming has decreased from about 8.6 million acres (3.5 million ha) in 1950 to 7 million acres (2.8 million ha) today. In the same period, the number of farms has dropped from about 270,000 to about 90,000. Many small farms have been sold to owners of larger

▲ *A family enjoys an outdoor meal during Midsummer celebrations on the island of Bergöklubben, in the Baltic Sea.*

CATTLE, 1995
(million head)

Country	Million head
Sweden	1.777
UK	11.868
USA	102.755
Australia	26.187
Denmark	2.06
Brazil	156.5

units, while, in other cases, farmland has been converted into forests or used for producing fast-growing trees for energy production.

Even so, food imports have shrunk from about 20 percent of total imports in the 1950s to 8 percent in the 1990s. The main reason for this is that productivity has been increased by mechanization and improved farming techniques. A more controversial cause is the increased use of ARTIFICIAL FERTILIZERS, PESTICIDES, and HERBICIDES.

Animal farming has changed more than any other sector of agriculture. As is true in many European countries, meat, milk, poultry, and eggs are produced by

▲ **Agricultural land on the shore of Lake Vättern, in the county of Småland, in southern Sweden.**

◀ **Dairy cattle on a traditional farm, near Uppsala, in central Sweden.**

KEY FACTS

● Production of meat, milk, dairy products, and eggs make up about two-thirds of the income of Swedish farmers.

● A typical Swedish farm is small with fewer than 50 acres (20 ha) of land. It employs only 1 person. Only about 10,000 farms are big enough to give full-time employment to 2 or more people.

● Food processing employs about 75,000 people. Most of it takes place in big units owned by the farmers, who have organized themselves in big COOPERATIVES for this purpose.

● Some farms near urban areas grow strawberries and black currants where people come to pick the fruit themselves. Other farmers welcome visitors and take in paying guests during the summer months. Farm visits are becoming very popular and give young people a chance to see what life is like in the country.

intensive, factory-farming methods. Most animals are kept indoors. Cows are fed artificial feed and milked mechanically, while many chickens and pigs are kept in battery cages and pens.

These production methods and the intensive use of chemicals have been condemned by many consumers. Because of this, there is a move toward more environmentally friendly practices and a return to traditional farming methods. Farmers are letting their cows into meadows to graze more often, and some farms are producing eggs from free-range hens. Other organic farms specialize in growing cereals and vegetables without the use of any chemicals.

Some land, especially on the island of Gotland and in northern Sweden, that was once used for growing crops, has been converted into pasture for sheep. Herding reindeer for meat and skins is still important to the economy of some 2,500 Lapp people,

in 51 villages in the northern part of Sweden. Animals either graze in the lowland forest areas or are moved between mountain slopes in the summer and forest areas in the winter, in search of good pastures. Today herdsmen use snow scooters and helicopters to drive their animals, whereas, traditionally, Lapps traveled on skis.

The most important agricultural areas are located in the plains of southern Sweden, where more than half of all farmland is to be found. Wheat and oilseed are the main crops in this region. There are also areas in the south that specialize in the production of fruit and vegetables. Farther north, where the climate is less favorable, crops for fodder and potatoes are more important.

Small farmers often have other jobs besides agriculture. Especially in the north and in the southern highlands, forestry is a common secondary occupation. Others

◀ *In a coastal village, fish hang to dry. This is a traditional way of preserving the catch, far removed from the big processing plants of the modern fishing industry.*

have taken up part-time work.

Although Swedish food production has become very efficient in the postwar era, production costs are expensive. Because of this, any surplus products are difficult to sell on the international market, because prices are high. Parliament has, therefore, decided to give incentives to farmers who choose to reduce their cereal and milk production. Not everyone agrees with this policy, because it is likely to result in more movement from villages to towns.

Fishing is mainly carried out from ports along the west coast and in the Baltic Sea.

▼ *A fruit and vegetable market in Malmö, the largest city in the major agricultural area of Skåne, in southern Sweden.*

Herring is the most important catch. The number of full-time fishermen has dropped from about 20,000 in 1950 to 4,000 today. Fishing accounts for only about 0.1 percent of Sweden's GROSS DOMESTIC PRODUCT (GDP), but it is important to people in coastal villages and to those living along the shores of the larger lakes.

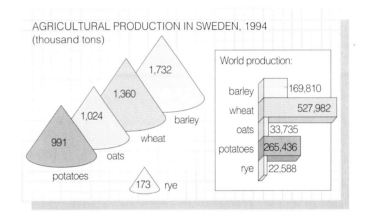

AGRICULTURAL PRODUCTION IN SWEDEN, 1994
(thousand tons)

1,732 barley
1,360 wheat
1,024 oats
991 potatoes
173 rye

World production:

barley	169,810
wheat	527,982
oats	33,735
potatoes	265,436
rye	22,588

Sweden is a highly industrialized country, and the export of manufactured products is extremely important for its economy. Even so, more people are employed in trade and services than in factories. Because the production processes in so many factories have become AUTOMATED, the number of industrial employees has dropped sharply during the last few decades. Only one Swede out of five is employed by an industrial company compared to almost one in two about the time of 1950.

This is because Sweden, where labor is expensive, has been facing increasing competition from countries where labor is cheap. This has led to the increasing use of sophisticated machinery in Swedish factories. Today computers and industrial

▲ *With an industrial tradition dating back to the 16th century, the town of Ludvika is still an important manufacturing center. Asea Brown Bovery (ABB), which makes generators and industrial robots, is the major employer.*

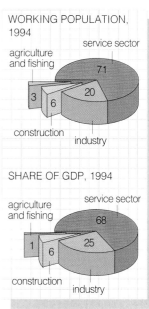

WORKING POPULATION, 1994

service sector
agriculture and fishing
71
3 6 20
construction industry

SHARE OF GDP, 1994

service sector
agriculture and fishing
68
1 6 25
construction industry

robots have taken over many jobs that previously were done manually. The high cost of labor has even forced some large companies, such as Volvo and Ericsson, to transfer the manufacture of some parts of their cars and telephones to other countries.

Industries that require a lot of manual labor, like the manufacture of clothing, are now becoming less important. Factories have shifted from making simple products to manufacturing more complex products, such as sophisticated machinery and electrical and electronic equipment. Highly qualified and skilled employees are needed to manufacture these goods. Telecommunication systems and mobile telephones, cars and heavy vehicles, power generators, and industrial robots are just some of the major products of Swedish engineering companies.

Other important industrial products are

KEY FACTS

● More than 500,000 people are employed in Swedish-owned companies outside of Sweden, while 200,000 people are employed in Sweden by foreign-owned companies.

● Sweden's most important trading partners are Germany, the U.K., the United States, and Japan.

● A high number of Swedish industrial workers are employed in large factories. Some 35% work for companies with more than 500 employees and only 6% in units with 20 people or less.

● Foreign investors own about a quarter of the value of shares registered on the Stockholm stock exchange.

● It is vital for Sweden, like most other small countries, to be able to sell large quantities of goods abroad. This is why Sweden is a strong supporter of free trade.

◀ *Inhalers for asthmatic patients are one of a wide range of products from the leading medical company Astra. Its main production units are in Södertälje, a city south of Stockholm.*

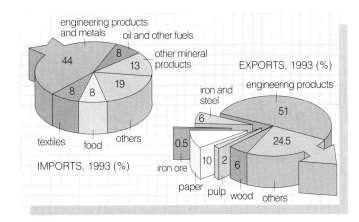

engineering products and metals 44
oil and other fuels 8
other mineral products 13
19
8
8
textiles
food
others

IMPORTS, 1993 (%)

EXPORTS, 1993 (%)

engineering products 51
iron and steel 6
24.5
iron ore 0.5
paper 10
pulp 2
wood 6
others

submarines, and guns for its own military forces as well as for export. But the export of arms is a very controversial issue. Many people feel that it contradicts the importance the Swedish government and people place on promoting international peace.

Despite recent economic problems, Sweden is still an important industrial country. One reason for the success of its products is a tradition of industrial innovation. Alfred Nobel, who made a fortune from inventing dynamite, is probably the best known Swede. This is because of the world-famous Nobel Prize that is financed by money from his business activities. In recent years,

medicines, ball bearings, and high-quality steel. Paper, produced in modern automated mills, has, to a large extent, replaced the export of pulp. Sweden also has its own defense industry, producing fighter bombers,

◀ *A woman worker on the production line of Saab Automobile. This company is the second largest Swedish car manufacturer after Volvo.*

▲ **The Swedish air force's most modern plane is the Saab Gripen. It has been offered for sale to several other countries.**

furniture from Ikea, clothes from Hennes & Mauritz, and packaging from Tetra Pak are examples of Swedish products that started on a small scale with a simple idea and grew to become internationally well known.

Today most Swedes are employed in the service sector, in hospitals, schools, stores, banks, and the transportation industry. Service industries have expanded rapidly since the 1950s. Together with public administration, they employ about 3 million people, compared to 800,000 in industry.

In the late 1990s, the number of people working in the PUBLIC SERVICE SECTOR has been reduced because of lack of money. Some activities in the areas of health and transportation have been taken away from local government agencies and given to private companies to run.

The fact that the number of people employed in industry and the public service sector has dropped is one reason unemployment is rising. More than 10 percent of the workforce was out of work in the late 1990s. About half of those laid off were invited to join government training programs aimed at teaching them the skills needed in order to work in modern industry.

The government has tried other ways of reducing unemployment. It is encouraging young people to go on to university, and offering early retirement packages to the older employees. Trade unions have demanded shorter working hours, and they have, in some cases, managed to negotiate small reductions. Also companies have asked for tax reductions as a way to increase employment.

TRANSPORTATION

Sweden has a well-developed transportation system. This is important in a country where urban centers are considerable distances apart. With high-speed trains, improved air transportation, and the construction of better roads, traveling time has been dramatically cut for today's travelers, and industrial products can now be moved more swiftly. This benefits large companies, such as car manufacturers, that make components in one place and assemble them in another.

In the 1990s a number of fast trains, the X-2000s, were built for use between major cities. They run at a speed of 124 miles per hour (200 kph). This is slower than the super-fast Japanese and French trains, but these Swedish-made trains can

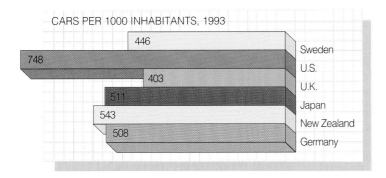

CARS PER 1000 INHABITANTS, 1993

446	Sweden
748	U.S.
403	U.K.
511	Japan
543	New Zealand
508	Germany

▼ *High-speed trains, the X-2000s, now connect major cities, cutting the former traveling time in half.*

▲ *At Slussen, in Stockholm, there are connections between all forms of transportation: trains, cars, buses, subway trains, and ferries.*

use existing tracks. This makes their construction cheaper. The train itself, not the track, tilts when it runs through a bend.

After a period of decline, the railroad system is being extended. This will make travel easier for people in the cities of the industrial belt west of Stockholm and in the northern coastal areas.

Air transportation is still, however, the easiest way to travel around Sweden. A journey from Stockholm to Kiruna that will

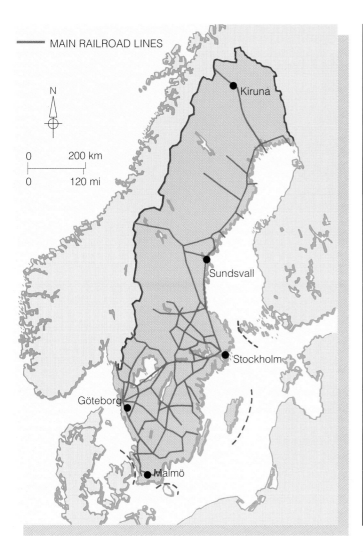

MAIN RAILROAD LINES

N

| 0 | 200 km |
| 0 | 120 mi |

Kiruna

Sundsvall

Stockholm

Göteborg

Malmö

take 18 to 20 hours by train can be done by plane in about three hours, including travel to and from the airports.

The train and road systems are linked to the outside world by ferries carrying cars, trucks, and sometimes railroad wagons to Finland, Denmark, Germany, England, and other countries. Smaller ferries take passengers and cars to Gotland and the other islands. Some ports are kept open in the winter by ice breakers. Snow and ice can make winter transportation difficult. Severe blizzards can block roads and stop rail traffic. With the help of big snow plows, traffic is kept going in all but the worst conditions.

▼ *A Stockholm underground station. The surface of the rock has been left in its natural state by the architect.*

In Sweden, as is true in most industrial countries, the environment has suffered as a result of rapidly growing industries and towns. Land was cleared to make room for towns to expand, and for new factories and shopping centers to be built. Between the 1850s and 1950s, factories were constructed, rivers were dammed, and roads were built. Little thought was given to the damage that was being done to the environment.

Only during the last quarter of a century have the Swedes made a serious effort to protect the environment and to stop the discharging of hazardous waste by industries, agriculture, and road traffic. They are only now beginning to realize how difficult and costly it will be to reverse some of the damage that has already been done.

Fortunately, there is still plenty of unspoiled countryside left in Sweden. Because of this, the environmental damage might not be as visible as it is in many other countries. However, dams have been built on most of the larger rivers to produce hydroelectricity. There has been irreparable destruction of sensitive forests in some mountain areas. Highways now cut through the once-pristine landscape, and towns are spreading into land that used to be fertile agricultural fields.

In the big cities, the worst problem is air pollution caused by cars and by boilers used for central heating. In spite of stricter controls over the type of fuel that is allowed, there has been little improvement because the number of cars has continued to increase.

Industrial discharge from factories has dropped considerably in recent years. New laws have made factories treat waste water before it is discharged into rivers, lakes, or into the public drainage system. The public sewage system has also been dramatically improved. Many polluted lakes have now been cleaned up as a result of these measures.

Swedish farmers use far fewer chemicals than their counterparts in some other European countries. Even so, harmful

◀ *A wolverine, one of many protected wild animals that lives in the north of Sweden. Because it kills reindeer, there is a conflict of interest between the reindeer-herding Lapps and animal conservationists.*

▶ *A swimmer diving into Lake Mälaren from the stairs of the City Hall in Stockholm. Water quality has improved greatly since a modern sewage system has been installed in all the suburbs and other cities around the lake.*

substances from agriculture have had an effect on the countryside. Traces of pesticides have been fatal to fish and to other creatures. Fertilizers leak into lakes, rivers, and the ocean. This encourages the growth of algae, which uses up the oxygen in water. Because of this, there are fewer fish in the Baltic Sea and along the west coast than there used to be.

The environmental problems in the Baltic Sea are, to a large extent, caused by other countries, especially by waste from Russia, the Baltic states, and Poland. Before the breakup of the Soviet Union, the Communist government paid little or no attention to environmental issues. Today Swedish and other Scandinavian experts are working with officials in these countries to try to reduce industrial pollution and clean up the environment. The main reason for this is that any help given now should benefit Sweden itself in the future.

The unsafe conditions of the nuclear power plants in Russia are of particular concern to Sweden. Since the nuclear catastrophe in Chernobyl in 1986, which affected parts of Sweden badly, Swedish experts have been helping local engineers to improve the safety in these installations.

The use of nuclear power has been a major issue in Sweden, ever since the first commercial reactor was started up in 1972. The subject has been widely debated. In a

KEY FACTS

● There are 24 national parks and about 1,400 nature preserves in Sweden. The largest parks are located in the north. One of these covers as much as 1,930 square miles (5,000 sq km). The parks and preserves make up 6% of the land area.
● In Sweden, 4% of all industrial investment is spent on measures aimed at improving the environment.
● One-half of the paper and 59% of the glass is recycled in Sweden.
● Swedish carbon dioxide emissions stand at 6.6 tons per capita (per head). This is about a third of that of the United States (19.1) but well above the world average of 4.0. In the U.K., it is 9.8; in India, 0.9; in China, 2.3; and in the United Arab Emirates, 33.9.

GREENHOUSE GAS EMISSIONS, 1993
(thousand tons)

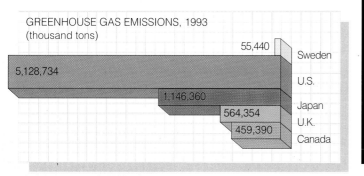

55,440	Sweden
5,128,734	U.S.
1,146,360	Japan
564,354	U.K.
459,390	Canada

◀ Environment-alists protest against the use of poisonous chemical materials during the digging of a tunnel for a new railroad line. The tunnel will cut through a mountain in Båstad, in southern Sweden.

referendum held in 1980, the voters gave a guarded yes to the use of this source of energy in the short term. On this basis, Parliament decided to allow 12 reactors to remain until the year 2010. Later, it was decided that one of these reactors would be shut down in 1998. No date has, as of yet, been set for the shutdown of the others. Those who think that this should be done as soon as possible claim that energy is now being wasted because it is cheap. Others, who want the reactors to remain in use, say that the alternative to nuclear power is energy from coal and oil. They argue that these are even more harmful to nature than nuclear power.

✚ THE FUTURE

For centuries Sweden was a relatively isolated country. In the 20th century, with the development of modern systems of communications, Sweden has drawn closer to the rest of the world. At the same time, fast trains, telephone links, and computers connected to the Internet have made communications within the country easier. Communications between the north and south of the country used to be difficult and slow. Now they are almost as easy as those between east and west.

Politically, Sweden moved closer to Europe when it became a member of the EU in 1995. Since the collapse of communism in the Soviet Union and Poland, it has become very important for Sweden that the Baltic Sea area remains

KEY FACTS

● By the year 2010, 1 out of 4 Swedes will be above the retiring age of 65. A huge fund has been created to safeguard the pension system.
● New sources of energy will have to be found by the year 2010 to replace Sweden's outdated nuclear reactors.
● Sweden is one of the 13 member countries of the European Space Agency (ESA). One of the ESA's projects is the European Space Programme. This has a ground station, called Esrange, near the town of Kiruna, north of the Arctic Circle. From there, space rockets are launched to study the atmosphere, including a phenomenon called the NORTHERN LIGHTS. It is part of a program of peaceful space research that started in 1975.

as stable as possible. The government is working closely with neighboring countries to secure peace in this area, to speed up economic development in the former Soviet republics, and to improve the environment. Because of pressure from Sweden, a council of cooperation, with all the Baltic Sea states as its members, has been set up.

For decades Swedes have enjoyed a high standard of living. More recently they have also become used to the sophisticated technology that has moved into many homes.

However, there have also been some problems. The welfare state, which has developed since the 1930s, is in trouble.

◀ *A scientist studies data on the Northern Lights, an atmospheric phenomenon normally only seen in latitudes close to the Arctic Circle. During periods of magnetic storms, this beautiful sight can be seen in central and even southern Sweden. It is important for scientists to understand how it works, because it can disturb radio communications.*

▶ *A rocket is launched at the space center Esrange, near Kiruna.*

With an unemployment rate of about 10 percent and an increasing number of retired citizens collecting pension, the burden of taxation has become too great for those who are working. Because of this, Parliament has decided to cut some of the social benefits to which Swedes have grown accustomed.

At the same time, Sweden looks to the future. Because it is a small country, Sweden tries to promote international cooperation in the field of science. The government also emphasizes research and innovation, so that the country will be able to keep pace with other well-developed industrial countries.

FURTHER INFORMATION

● THE EMBASSY OF SWEDEN
1501 M Street, NW
Washington, D.C. 20005

● SWEDISH TRADE COUNCIL
150 North Michigan Avenue, Suite 1200
Chicago, IL 60601-7594
1-888-ASK SWEDEN

● SWEDISH TRAVEL AND TOURISM
COUNCIL
P.O. Box 4649 Grand Central Station
New York, NY 10163-4649

BOOKS ABOUT SWEDEN

Carlson, Bo Kage. *Sweden*. Austin, TX:
Thomson Learning, 1995.

McNair, Sylvia. *Sweden*. Children's Press,
1998.

Rabe, Monica. *Sweden*. Gareth Stevens,
1998.

Zickgraf, Ralph. *Sweden*. Chelsea House,
1997.

GLOSSARY

ARTIFICIAL FERTILIZERS
Chemicals that are added to soil to help
crops grow.

AUTOMATED
When machinery is operated by computer-
controlled processes or robots rather than
by people.

COOPERATIVE
A group of people who work together,
rather than as individuals, sharing the
costs of production and the profits.

GROSS DOMESTIC PRODUCT (GDP)
The total value of all the goods and
services produced by a country in a year.

HERBICIDES
Chemicals that are used by farmers
to kill weeds growing among crops.

ICE AGE
A period of time when ice sheets and
glaciers advanced from the polar regions
to cover areas that had previously had a

warmer climate. The last ice age ended
in about 8,000 B.C., when the ice finally
retreated to its present position.

NORTHERN LIGHTS
This is an atmospheric phenomenon
(sometimes known as the aurora borealis).
It occurs when electrons that are rich
in energy from the sun hit oxygen and
nitrogen atoms in the upper atmosphere.

PESTICIDES
Chemicals that kill insects that are harmful
to farmers' crops.

PUBLIC SERVICE SECTOR
Elements of the service sector, such as
hospitals and social services, that are
financed by a government. These may
vary from country to country.

SUSTAINABLE FORESTS
Forests where fast-growing trees are
continuously being replanted to replace
those that have been harvested.

INDEX

© Macdonald Young Books
1999

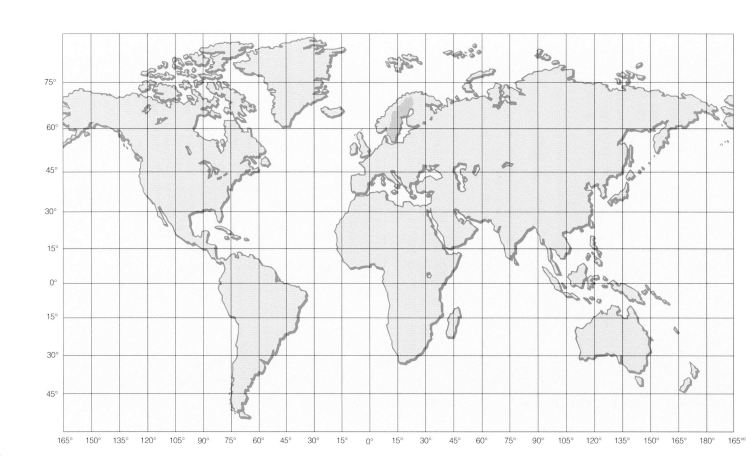